LETTING GO

An Allegory

David W. Ballard

ACKNOWLEDGMENTS

Jesus Christ, Mom, John Waller, Lisa Gambill, Caleb Ballard, Ellie Ballard, Bailey Ballard

In memory of Martha Malling
because you never stopped loving

Every spring, a magical tree sitting on a grassy mount grew special leaves. The name of the tree was Pater, and he saw to it that his leaves grew according to different kinds.

There was Aspen, Birch, Maple, Magnolia, Fir, and so on. Even though there were numerous types of leaves hanging from Pater's branches, they all spoke one unique leaf language amongst themselves.

The leaves' affection for Pater ran deep, and they were his crowning glory. He called to them often to warn them of dangerous storms and anything that might get in their way or cause them trouble.

One leaf named Green was the brightest of the bunch. He got his name because from the time he was a bud, he had the same rich color as the stem of a new tulip rising through the earth. When the sun shone through him, you could see the dark veins that ran through the course of his lush, green body.

Green enjoyed playing with the other magical leaves, especially during April's showers. Cool gusts of wind would blow light rain in the warm air, allowing Green and the other leaves to play games as they rustled about, flapped around, and turned over.

To Green, the only thing better than playing these leaf games was spending time with his best friend Maple. The two never wrestled in the wind or played hard, physical games, but they loved to sunbathe together under clear, sunny skies.

All that spring and summer, they talked about life in the tree while watching the sun rise and set, rise and set, as the warm seasons drifted into fall.

At the outset of one fall day, Green and the other leaves were wrestling when suddenly Green's friend, Aspen, fell from Pater and fluttered to the ground.

Green was at a loss: what was going on? This wasn't the way their games were supposed to go.

"Aspen just fell!" Green exclaimed. "What do we do now?"

But no one knew. This was the first time any of the leaves had fallen.

Green called to Pater, "How do we get Aspen back in his place again?"

"We can't, Green," Pater said. "Aspen fell to the ground because all of you leaves fall; it's part of your nature."

"Not mine," Green said. "I love being here with you and all my leaf friends. I'll never leave."

"I'm sorry, Green, but someday you will fall, and so will all your dear friends," Pater said.

"Why?" Green asked.

"Because I made you to take the world's sparse and polluted nature and make it full and clean again; and to share nature's life cycle, to show its passing beauty."

But Green didn't listen; he just wanted to windsurf and play leaf games with his friends.

So he did just that.

But one fall day, everything around Green seemed to take on an unreal quality. He couldn't quite put a vein to it, but all the leaves were changing colors: some from green to red, while others to orange, yellow, and purple. Green fought this change and tried to keep his color, but the cold weather was having its way with him and darkening his body.

So, he pointed out his observations to Maple. "Maple, I'm not completely green anymore! What's happening to me?"

"I don't know, Green, but maybe we're turning colors for a reason."

"Oh, yeah, and what's that?"

"Like Pater said: to show nature's life cycle and how it can be beautiful."

"Is that why you look so pretty, Maple?"

"You've always had a way with words, Green."

"Maple, please stay with me. I can't lose you, too."

"I'll stay with you as long as it takes," Maple said.

But the weather grew even colder, and more of Green's friends fell from Pater's limbs. Then one frigid day, Green was playing with his nearest neighbor, Birch, when Birch said, "I'm out, Green. I'll see you on the other side."

"Come on, Birch, you know leaving is for losers," Green said.

But Birch silently drifted past Green to the ground.

"Birch was a fool," Green said to Pater.

"No, he wasn't," Pater said. "He was only following his nature."

"Well, I won't," Green said.

But Green's fellow leaves continued to fall until there were none left but Maple and himself.

The scene was hard to take. Everything appeared dead. Pater was leafless now and had taken the form of a skeleton, a shell of his former self. Meanwhile, the grass looked like dead men's yellowing beards growing from the ground. Even the flowers had lost their bloom, all from winter's bitter, cold snaps.

So, Green just stared off into the distance in a haze. He thought: If only there was something he could do to stop time and go back to when he was young. But no matter what he did, the wintry weather remained, and the feel of it only reminded him of all his aches and pains.

Maple said, "Green, shouldn't we listen to Pater and fall to the ground as the others have? Isn't that what we're supposed to do?"

"No, Maple. This is our home."

"I know, but we can't stay here forever."

"You're not giving up and leaving me too, are you?"

"I'm not giving up," she said. "It's just my time to go."

Green stiffened. "Come on, Maple! Don't leave me like this."

"Like what? Coarse and brown; cranky and bitter; defiant and critical? You've got to give up those things, Green. Pater had it right. It's in our nature to fall."

"But..." Green searched for the right words to say, but all he could produce was one final plea. "Maple, I love you. If you loved me, too, you'd stay."

"I love you, too, Green, but that's why I must go. I can't stand to see you this way anymore."

Green turned away.

"Don't worry," Maple said. "I'll see you again even if it's from afar."

In one fluid motion, Maple unburdened herself and fell from her place on Pater's limb. "I love you, Maple," Green called after her, but he couldn't tell if she heard him as she sailed to the ground. Now that she was gone, his parting words seemed empty, deadening him even more.

Green said to himself, "Great, my best friend is gone. Now it's just me." He gripped Pater even tighter.

That night, storms set in with flashes of purple lightning and peals of rumbling thunder, making Green tremble. Even the wind became an enemy, whistling around him, nearly pulling him from his limb. Truly, it had become a troubling thing to be alone in the tree, where windsurfing and playing with the other leaves was long past. Now it was all he could do to hang on and survive.

He kept fighting: "I won't fall. The others were weak."

But the self-talk was no comfort, so that night Green went to a dark place where he knew nothing and felt nothing. It was a fitful night as he wrestled with constant thoughts about falling.

The next morning, Green awoke to the sound of three young boys laughing. The boys were raking Green's friends into piles. All Green's leaf friends were there, making leaf-laughing sounds, because they were getting the chance to draw even closer together than they once had on Pater's limbs. It looked like such fun, but in a way, it was distant and remote, just as Green had become.

It was a curious thing though. Three young boys were laughing below Pater, and the smallest one was pointing in Green's general direction. "Hey guys, look at that leaf! He's the last one left on this tree. I wonder what he's still doing up there."

Right then, Pater chimed in, "Green, listen to me! You don't have to fight anymore. You can always let go."

"When will I know it's my time?" Green asked.

"When you accept your nature and submit and yield to me," Pater said.

Green didn't understand, but as he considered Pater's words, the boy reached up and touched Green. Pater stirred and a slight breeze kicked up. All at once, Green felt a sense of ease washing over his brittle, scarred body.

Green whispered to Pater, "Is this my time, Pater?"

Pater nodded in the wind. "Yes, my dear Green."

At that moment, Green realized that the passage of his life was short, yet still important, and necessary, even though it was about to end.

The weary leaf said, "Thank you for loving me, Pater, even when I didn't understand or trust what you were trying to teach me."

"I'm glad you know now that I always loved you."

"I do," Green said with such yielding submission that he lost himself into the magical tree, finally making a clean break from his dear friend.

As if anticipating Green's fall, the smallest boy caught Green and held him up with an outstretched hand for his friends to see. "I got him!"

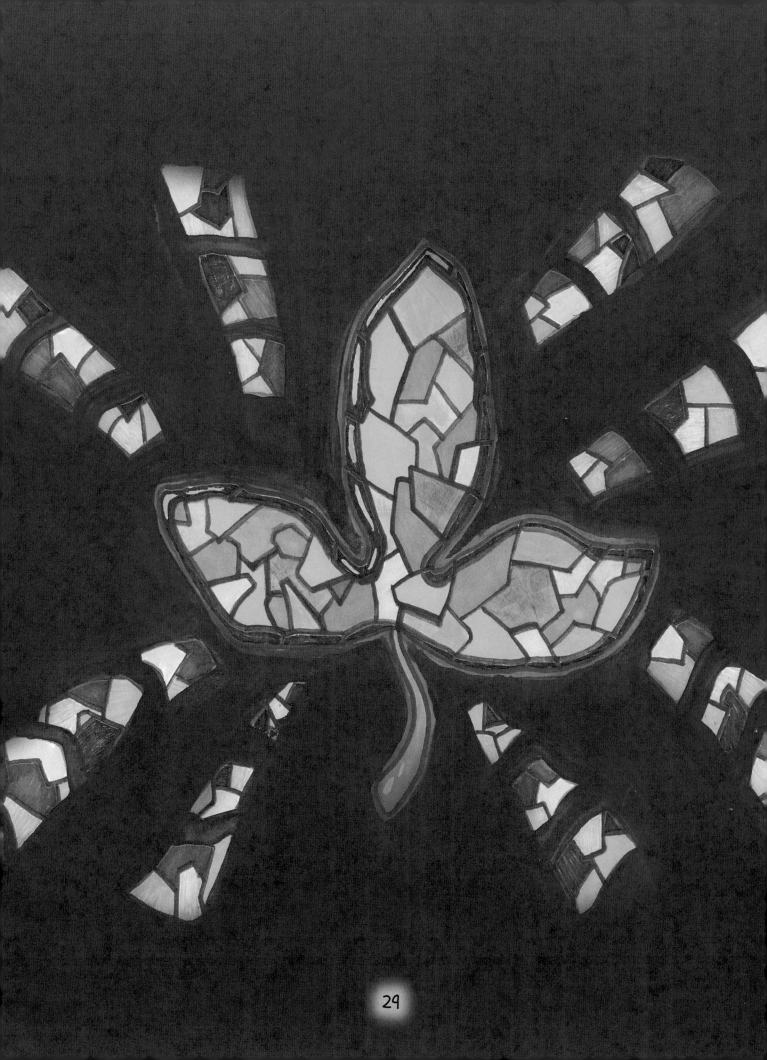

Finally, Green stopped thinking only about himself. Instead, he realized that by letting go, he wouldn't be bound to any one place or time, and for that reason, he could always share his story with anyone and everyone.

Made in the USA
Middletown, DE
23 October 2023

40607742R00020